UNIVERSITY OF HOUSTON SYSTEM
UNIVERSITY OF HOUSTON

RODOLFO J. CORTINA, PH.D.

Assistant Vice Chancellor for International Studies and
Programs, UH System
Assistant Vice President for Undergraduate Studies, UH
Division of Academic Affairs
Office of Undergraduate Studies

209 E Cullen Building
Houston, TX 77204-2036

(713) 743-9102 ■ Fax: (713) 743-9117
E-mail: rcortina@uh.edu ■ www.uh.edu

THE SECOND OTTOMAN CAPITAL

EDİRNE

A PHOTOGRAPHIC HISTORY

Engin Özendes

Republic of Turkey Ministry of Culture

yapı-endüstri merkezi yayınları

Republic of Turkey Ministry of Culture

This book has been prepared with the support of the Ministry of Culture.

FOREWORD

1999 is the 700th anniversary of the founding of the Ottoman Empire, whose spectacular history is full of remarkable achievements, particularly in the cultural sphere. Awareness of this very diverse cultural legacy is essential for the Turkish Republic today.

Within the scope of the celebrations of the 700th anniversary of the Ottoman Empire, our Ministry has lent its support to a series of books drawing on this cultural heritage published by the Architectural Foundation and Yapı-Endüstri Merkezi (The Building & Industry Center). We are proud to have contributed to the publication of these works focusing on Ottoman period architecture as part of the commemorative events marking the founding of the Ottoman Empire in 1299.

This book presents photographs of Edirne, second capital of the Ottoman Empire, in the late nineteenth and early twentieth centuries.

Illustrated by early photographs of buildings and urban landscapes which in many cases have been swallowed up by time today, this book brings Edirne as it was a century and more ago to life once more.

Other books published as part of the same series are as follows:

• *The First Ottoman Capital, Bursa* (English and Turkish), Engin Özendes

• *The Last Ottoman Capital, Istanbul* (English and Turkish), Engin Özendes

• *Ottoman Fountains* (English and Turkish)

In addition, the following four books have been published on the initiative of the aforementioned organisations, again as part of the commemorative events.

• *Tradition of the Turkish House and Safranbolu Houses* (English and Turkish), Reha Günay

• *Sinan the Architect and His Works*, Reha Günay

• *Kent ve Mimarlık Üzerine İstanbul Yazıları*, Doğan Kuban

• *Binaların Yeniden Kullanımı*, Ülkü Altınoluk

I congratulate the Architectural Foundation and Yapı-Endüstri Merkezi, and the esteemed authors of these books for their contribution to our cultural life.

İstemihan Talay
Minister of Culture

First Edition
YEM Yayın - August 1999

Coordinator
Sedat ACAR

Publishing Manager
Gülçin İPEK

Publishing Secretary
Dilşad AKTAŞ

Translated from the Turkish by
Priscilla Mary IŞIN

Realization
Kenan ÖZTÜRK

Layout
Ayfer TONUS

Cover Design
Tuncay BAYRAKTAR

Color Separation & Printed by
Doruk Grafik, Istanbul

YEM Yayın (Yapı-Endüstri Merkezi Yayınları)

Cumhuriyet Cad. 329 Harbiye 80230 İSTANBUL
Phone: (0212) 230 29 19 - 219 39 39 pbx
Fax: (0212) 248 48 14 - 225 66 23
e-mail: yem@yem.net   web: www.yem.net

ISBN: 975-7438-81-2
THE SECOND OTTOMAN CAPITAL EDİRNE

CONTENTS

PREFACE

In 1826 a Frenchman named Joseph Nicéphore Niépce succceeded in obtaining the first permanent image of the view from the window of his house in the city of Chalon after an exposure time lasting several hours. Following Niépce's death in 1833, his young partner Louis Jacques Mandé Daguerre carried on his research, and his discovery of photography, called the Daguerreotype, was proclaimed to the world by the French Academy of Sciences in 1839.

This French invention was introduced to the East by adventurers, writers, painters, architects and travellers in search of archaeological ruins. They were eager to capture the fascinating sights of the Orient already known to them from engravings through the eye of the newfangled camera, which produced pictures of reality itself. Apart from Istanbul, that city so different from those of the West, they photographed towns, cities and ancient ruins all over the Ottoman Empire. For those interested in the region's archaeological wealth, photography quickly became an indispensable tool.

As western travellers became more closely acquainted with this Muslim country, their interest in its society began to rival that in its ancient past. Human interest entered into their photographs, and now people were to be seen in front of monuments, in markets and bazaars and in the streets. Gradually photographic studios began to open in the major cities of the empire, and Ottoman photographers joined those from western countries. Studios multiplied and photography became widely known throughout the Ottoman lands. Photographs of people, not as accessories but for their own sake, became fashionable. Water sellers, butchers, barbers, sherbet sellers, chimney sweeps, boza sellers, porters and a host of other local figures were all depicted in their distinctive costumes.

As Ottoman photographers increased in number from the 1850s onwards, they began to open studios on the Grand' Rue de Péra, the famous main street through the westernised district of Péra north of the Golden Horn.

The name Péra dated from Byzantine times and meant 'opposite bank', in reference to the opposite shore of the Golden Horn facing the walled city of Istanbul proper. The Turks called this district Beyoğlu, and today the Grand' Rue de Péra has become İstiklal Caddesi.

In Edirne, second capital of the Ottoman Empire, studios were established by photographers such as Constantin Anghelides, E. Foscolo, D. Michailides, Miltiyadi, Aram Bardizban, Leonidas Nicolau, K. Panghelides and E. Popoff. Basile Kargopoulo, one of Istanbul's foremost studio photographers, opened a branch studio in Edirne, and subsequently went into partnership with the local Edirne photographer E. Foscolo. In addition other Istanbul photographers from time to time bought up negatives of photographs of Edirne from local photographers and made prints of these bearing their own names.

Publishing postcards of the city also became widespread. In the nineteenth century postcards of Edirne were published by Isaac J. Canetti, B. Vafiades, Jacques Saül, A. Ilieff and Joseph N. Mitrani, and in the early twentieth century by bookseller M. Şevki, Tüccarzade İbrahim Hilmi and F. Fettah. Following the Bulgarian occupation which began on 26 March 1913, Librairie Oltcheff and D. Bajdaroff produced postcards of Edirne in Sofya.

The nineteenth century marked the beginning of troubled times for Edirne, when former days of pride and prosperity were forgotten in a series of enemy occupations. Although Istanbul had succeeded Edirne as capital way back in the fifteenth century, the city had retained a privileged status over the intervening centuries, the sultan often moving his court here for months at a time. But now Edirne was both embattled and forgotten. It became guardpost of the fluctuating western frontier, and the first target of attacks on Anatolia. But even though its days of glory were forgotten, the magnificent view of the city from afar, its slender minarets pointing skywards, and the enchanting sight of Selimiye Mosque could not be erased.

When Bursa, first capital of the Ottoman Empire, handed on the baton to Edirne, was this only because the latter had been conquered? What were the events and developments which led up to the city being appointed capital? A wealth of material illustrating the changes in Edirne's urban texture in the form of photographs dating from the second half of the nineteenth and early twentieth centuries, introduced by an account of the earlier history of the city could help to throw light on the fascinating past of this city. So this book was born.

I wish to thank my friend Pierre de Gigord, who has always been so generous with his assistance, for kindly agreeing to bring together our collections of photographs for this book, and for his wholehearted interest in the project.

Engin Özendes, ESFIAP
Istanbul, 1999

LEGEND OF THE CITY

City of rivers

The Hebrus (today Meriç) grew in size and strength as it first joined the waters of the Artistkos (Arda). Rushing exuberantly along, it encountered the Tonzos (Tunca). At the confluence of these three great rivers, the river god listened to the gushing of the waters and witnessed the great ball of the sun brought by Helios from the East to warm the world. Things seemed to be going well until mutterings were added to the soothing sound of water. They explained to the river god what had happened.

Son of the dawn goddess, Boreas, who blew fierce winds and icy gales, lived in Thrace. He was a powerful creature with a flowing beard and huge wings. Descended from the Titans, he was as implacable and belligerent as they. That day black lowering clouds poured sheets of rain over the land, and tempestuous waves raged across the Aigaion Sea. As Boreas filled his lungs to blow over the land, he looked down for a moment and saw Oreithyia, daughter of the Athenai king Erechtheus, playing with her brothers and sisters by a small river. He fell in love with her at first sight. Naturally the god of the north wind could not love without possessing the object of his passion, and he descended like a whirlwind upon her, snatched her up in his red wings and carried her off to his cold home of Thrace.

The river god was delighted, because whenever he passed through this land Boreas used to blow with all his might, and the river god was obliged to set the waters of the Hebrus, Artistkos and Tonzos rivers boiling and rising in their turn. Then the foremost town of the Odyrs, people of the great god Odra, consort of the mother goddess, suffered damage. But this time Boreas had other things on his mind and no thought for torrential rain or gales. Upon hearing the good news the river god looked fondly towards Odrysai.

HISTORY OF THE CITY

The Odrys

Near the city of Ainos archaeologists have excavated a settlement belonging to one of the oldest known neolithic cultures in the Balkans. Their pottery and the defensive wall around the settlement are typical of contemporary Anatolian cultures, so these people are thought to have been a colony from Anatolia.

Later Thrace was settled by a people whose courage and skills as warriors put fear into many of their neighbours. These qualities meant that the Thracians were sought after as mercenaries by first the Athenians and then the Romans. Thracian settlements took many forms, from caves to strong forts, farms to fishing villages whose houses were raised on poles, and unwalled cities.

The Apsinti, east of Ainos, the Drugeri in the central region of the Hebrus, the Tyns in Salmydessos and the Kalopothaks were some of the Thracian tribes who inhabited the region stretching from Ainos to the Kallipolis (Gallipoli) peninsula. Most famous of all were the Odrys who at the height of their power inhabited an area extending from the Tonzos valley to the Aegean coast.

Odrysai was one of the major towns of the powerful Odrys Thracians. Odrysai lay in the fork at the confluence of the Hebrus and the Tonzos, and was a centre of commerce.

Transit point

Since this region lay on the only transit route between Europe and Asia Minor, migrations, invasions, trade and cultural exchange had a profound effect on its inhabitants. The passage of peoples to and fro was unceasing.

In 513 BC the Persian king Darius led his army against the Scythians, crossing the Bosphorus and advancing along the coast into Thrace. The army made its first stop in the land of the Odrys, which now became part of the Persian Empire.

Two decades later, in 492 BC, another Persian army led by Mardonius consolidated Persian rule over Thrace, and in 480 BC the Thracians were obliged to supply troops for the army of King Xerxes, who set out from the Gulf of Melas (today Saros) on the Kallipolis peninsula, and conquered his way to the city of Ainos, taking possession of the entire Hebrus plain.

After the Persians lost control of the region, the Thracian tribes resolved to unite, choosing as their leader King Teres of the Odrys. In this way the Odrys became master of an area stretching from the Hebrus to Kypsela (Ipsala) and Varna, and established an aristocratic feudal state.

The Roman period

In 342-341 BC the Odrys were defeated in battle against the Macedonian army led by King Philip, and thereafter steadily declined in power. When his father was killed in 336 BC Alexander the Great, afraid of uprisings tearing his country apart, marched into Thrace in 335 BC. He advanced along the coast, crossing through the kingless land of the Thracians and over the river Nestos (Mesta) to reach the foothills of the Balkans in just ten days. After passing through Odrysia and over the Hebrus, he marched along the banks of the Tonzos, then crossed a pass. After Alexander's death the successors to his empire turned Thrace into a satrapy.

In 280-279 BC Thrace was invaded by the Galatians, but the Odrys soon regained their former power and their king Kotys established friendly relations with Macedonia. In the war against Rome which lasted from 171-168 BC, Kotys was the only ally of Perseus. Eventually the Romans conquered Macedonia, while Thrace began to live in the shadow of Rome.

The Romans pursued a policy of maximising their influence over the region by establishing numerous kingdoms and principalities, but the Thracians who had never been amenable to foreign domination rebelled against all these efforts. Nevertheless, in the early years of our era, the land of the Odrys had become a Roman base and leverage point for maintaining its power over the region. In these years the Greek coastal cities became part of Rome, ruled by a Macedonian governor.

In 37-38 AD Caligula made Rhaimetalkes king of Thrace, but after Rhaimetalkes was killed the Emperor Claudius put an end to Thracian independence. In 45 AD Thrace was reduced to a province of the Roman Empire.

Hadrianopolis

When the Roman emperor Hadrian (117-138) travelled to the East in 123-124, he commanded that new buildings be constructed in the town of Odrysai, also known as Uscudama. The town grew into a city, and became one of the most important in the Roman Empire. It was now thought worthy to take the name of the emperor who had so honoured the city, and Odrysai was re-named Hadrianopolis (Adrianopolis), Hadrian's city.

The most important building which Hadrian had constructed here was the castle. Corresponding exactly to the plan of a Roman castrum, the castle had nine gates, four circular towers, one at each corner, and along each wall twelve quadrangular turrets. Around the walls was a moat. When Rome was enjoying its golden age during the second century and first half of the third century, the cities of Thrace grew and prospered. Hadrianopolis, an important military stronghold and centre of trade with a fertile hinterland, was no exception.

In 297 Diocletian (284-305) established a tetrarchy to govern the Roman Empire more effectively in these times of civil strife, and the empire was divided into East and West, Diocletian becoming emperor of the former. As part of these changes Hadrianopolis was made provincial capital of Haemimontus, one of six provinces in Thrace. But when Diocletian abdicated in 305 a power struggle broke out between the eastern and western empires.

In 324 a battle was fought near Hadrianopolis in which Licinius, emperor of eastern Rome, was defeated by Constantine, emperor of the West. Licinius withdrew to Byzantium, but was again defeated and then killed. Constantine moved the capital from Rome to Byzantium, where as Constantine I he ruled the now reunited Roman Empire alone from 324 until 337. The new capital was known as Nea Roma until Constantine renamed it Constantinopolis after himself on 11 May 330.

In 378 during the reign of the Emperor Valens (364-378) a Roman army was defeated in battle against the Goths north of Hadrianopolis.

In order to prevent upheavals in Thrace and a threatened mass exodus out of the region, the Emperor Theodosius I (379-395) adopted a more conciliatory policy towards the Goths. Theodosius spent September of 381 in Hadrianopolis.

Fifty years of relative peace was broken by a new threat, as the Huns launched incursions against Thrace. The looting and plundering continued sporadically between 441 and 447.

In 550 it was the turn of the Avars, who roundly beat a Byzantine army outside Hadrianopolis. Huge numbers of soldiers were taken captive and the sacred standard of Constantine the Great was seized by the Avars. The victors pursued the Byzantines as far as the wall of Anastasius west of Constantinople, but here the Byzantines re-formed, set upon the Avars and recaptured both the sacred standard and some of their companions from the enemy.

During the reign of Heraclius (610-641), whose Heraclian dynasty lasted until the end of the seventh century, Hadrianopolis was the centre of five bishoprics.

In 807 the Emperor Nicephorus I (802-811) led an army against the Bulgars, who had taken Hadrianopolis, and recaptured the city, but had to immediately return to Constantinople where an uprising was being fomented against him.

From 1018 onwards, the Pecheneks posed the greatest threat to Byzantine security. During the reign of Constantine IX Monomachus (1042-1055) the Pecheneks united to raise a powerful army which marched to Hadrianopolis, encamped beneath its walls, and commenced raiding and looting the surrounding villages and towns. When Constantinople was captured by the Latins in 1204, Hadrianopolis came under the control of Venice, which received the larger share of the divided Byzantium.

In 1336 one of the daughters of Andronicus III (1328-1341) married the Bulgarian prince Mikhael in Hadrianopolis. When Andronicus III died in 1341, he was succeeded by his nine-year-old son John V (1341-1391). Cantacuzene, who had been entrusted with the post of regent, betrayed this trust on 26 October 1341 by declaring himself emperor in Didymoteikhos. The resulting conflict between factions supporting John V and Cantacuzene escalated into civil war, which broke out in Hadrianopolis and swiftly spread through Thrace. Cantacuzene took Hadrianopolis and in 1347 entered Constantinople, where for the second time he proclaimed himself emperor as John VI in place of John V Palaeologus. In 1352 he was obliged to fight for possession of Hadrianopolis once again, this time against John V, who was strongly supported by the Serbians and Bulgarians, including a contingent of 4000 cavalry. Cantacuzene appealed for help against this intimidating force from the Turkish sultan Orhan Gazi (1326-1360), who was at the same time his son-in-law. Orhan Gazi sent his old friend and ally a force of around ten thousand soldiers under Süleyman Bey, so securing Cantacuzene's victory.

THE OTTOMAN PERIOD

Hadrianopolis becomes Edirne

One night in 1354 Süleyman Bey took the fortress of Kallipolis, opening the way for the Ottoman advance into Thrace. In 1360 under Orhan Gazi's successor Murad I (1359-1389) Turkish forces conquered Didymotheikos. Murad I set his sights on expanding Ottoman territory into Europe, and quickly took Sultan, Çorlu and Keşan in western Thrace. He charged Lala Şahin Paşa with the conquest of Hadrianopolis, and together with another Turkish commander Hacı İlbeyi the city was captured from the Byzantines in July 1362.

In the *fetihname* (declaration of conquest) sent by Murad I to Üveys Han, ruler of the Turkish Celayirli principality, Hadrianople is referred to as Edirne. In 1363 Murad I paid a visit to his new city, and appointed Lala Şahin Paşa commander of the garrison. Edirne became a crucial military base for subsequent territorial conquests by the Turks in Rumelia (Land of the Romans) as they called the Balkans and Thrace. The following year the Battle of Sırpsındığı was fought 25 km west of Edirne against a joint army of Serbs, Wallachians and Hungarians.

One night Sultan Murad had a dream in which he was conversing with a wise, white bearded old man, who advised him to build a palace in Edirne. Murad I took heed of this dream and constructed himself a large palace beside the river.

The Ottoman Dar-ül Mülk

Following the conquest large numbers of Turks began to settle in Edirne, which was proclaimed the Ottoman capital in 1365, marking a new chapter in its history. It was from here that Sultan Bayezid I (1389-1403) commanded the first Turkish siege of Constantinople.

After the death of Yıldırım Bayezid I, the empire was torn apart by a decade of strife between his sons who all laid claim to the throne. During the interregnum, which lasted from 1403 to 1413, Edirne acquired even more importance. Bayezid's eldest son Emir Süleyman Çelebi moved the state treasury from Bursa to Edirne, where he declared himself sultan. In 1411, his brother Musa Çelebi, with the help of the voyvode of Wallachia, attacked the city and seized it from his brother. Musa Çelebi struck coins in his own name. In 1413 Mehmed I Çelebi (1413-1421) reunited the country and took Edirne from his brother.

In 1419, another claimant to the throne made a sudden appearance, declaring himself to be Mustafa Çelebi (Mustafa the Pretender), the son of Bayezid I who had disappeared at the Battle of Ankara against Tamerlane. Gathering an army of supporters he captured Edirne and struck money in his name. Later he marched into Anatolia, but was defeated by Murad II (1421-1451) near Bursa. Mustafa Çelebi, who had made off with his father's treasury but been waylaid on his way to Wallachia, was brought back to Edirne in 1442 and executed. The first public festival was held in the city in the wake of this event.

Murad II also held magnificent celebrations in Edirne upon the circumcision of his sons Alaeddin and Mehmed. In 1444 Murad II abdicated in favour of his son Mehmed so as to lead a life of peaceful retirement in Manisa. Mehmed II was the first Ottoman sultan whose accession took place in Edirne after the city became the Ottoman capital. The future Mehmed the Conqueror was just a child of 12 when his father entrusted him with the throne, but Murad II's retirement did not last long. When a crusader army gathered against the Ottoman Empire he was obliged to return to Edirne and resume leadership of the army against the enemy.

Murad II crushed the enemy at Varna, and attempted again to leave the country to his son, but this time the janissaries mutinied, and he had to return to Edirne again to take up his throne for the third time. Only upon his death on 5 February 1451 did his son Mehmed II (1451-1481) finally rule independently. This young man of 19 had a very important goal ahead of him, to take Constantinople, and he began his preparations in Edirne.

Constantinople becomes capital

Mehmed II achieved his greatest ambition in 1453. In a final attack on the morning of 29 May, the landward walls of Constantinople were breached. That day the young sultan rode into the city and performed his prayers in the great church of Haghia Sophia. He was to go down in history as Fatih Sultan Mehmed, Mehmed the Conqueror. Constantinople became the third Ottoman capital, but Edirne was not pushed altogether into the background, and was the scene of many important events in the empire's subsequent history. Mehmed II's son Bayezid II (1481-1512) had Gedik Ahmed Paşa executed at Edirne Palace, and it was here that the struggle with his son Selim for the throne took place.

Edirne was the main military base for all the sixteenth century campaigns of conquest westwards into Europe, and in consequence the sultans spent much of their time in the palace there. So Edirne was effectively the seat of government for much of that time, enjoying the attention that this brought. Yavuz Sultan Selim I (1512-1520), Süleyman I the Magnificent (1520-1566) and Selim II (1566-1574) all founded public buildings here.

Edirne's golden age

In the 17th century, beginning with Ahmed I (1603-1617), the sultans continued to divide their time between Istanbul and Edirne. Osman II (1617-1622) and Murad IV (1623-1640) organised magnificent hunting parties in the forests around Edirne, and Mehmed IV (1649-1687), so passionately fond of the chase that he was known as Mehmed the Hunter, spent most of his time hunting here. In the 1670s this sultan embarked on his campaigns against Russia and Poland from this surrogate capital.

Another sultan who preferred life in Edirne to Istanbul was Mustafa II (1695-1703), who was deposed after an uprising known as the Edirne Incident in 1703.

Following the Battle of Prut against Russia, which ended in the Treaty of Prut signed on 16 April 1712, the Russians refused to withdraw from Poland as agreed. After seven months the Ottomans resolved to go to war again, and Ahmed III (1703-1730) set off at the head of his army from Istanbul to Edirne. Alarmed by this, Peter I of Russia sent news that he was ready to negotiate. As a result of peace talks held in Edirne the Treaty of Edirne was signed on 24 June 1713, under which the Russians agreed to withdraw from Poland within two months, to the restoration of the frontiers as they had stood in the reign of Mehmed IV, and to the return of King Karl XII of Sweden -who had been living in exile in the Ottoman Empire- to his country under the escort of a Turkish guard detachment.

Destruction and decline

First the great fire of 1745 and then the earthquake of 1751 left Edirne devastated. Its days of popularity and splendour were gone, and the city went into decline.

The leading Ottoman notables in the Balkans, afraid of their power being undermined when Selim III (1789-1807) established his new army the Nizam-ı Cedit, rebelled twice in Edirne, in 1801 and 1806.

War broke out with Russia in 1828, and on 22 August 1829 the Russians took Edirne after a siege of just three days, forcing the Ottomans to sign a peace treaty that would leave the empire weakened. The treaty was signed on 14 September 1829 and Edirne restored to Ottoman rule, but the Muslim population felt vulnerable and began to abandon the city in large numbers. Sultan Mahmud II (1808-1839) visited the city in 1831 to boost its morale, remaining for ten days during which he gave orders for the rebuilding of the city's damaged buildings. In commemoration of the visit coins bearing the stamp of Edirne were struck, the three denominations being known as the hayriye, nısfiye and rubiye.

During the Ottoman-Russian War of 1877-1878 Edirne was again occupied by Russian forces on 20 January 1878. This time the occupation lasted for over 13 months, during which many areas of the city were burnt and razed before Ottoman rule was restored on 13 March 1879.

Three decades of relative peace for Edirne again came to an end when the Balkan states formed an alliance against the Ottoman Empire and war broke out in 1912. A Bulgar and Serbian army attacked Edirne, whose defending forces under Şükrü Paşa held out for 160 days until hunger forced them to surrender on 26 March 1913.

On 22 July 1913 an Ottoman force led by Enver Paşa met with no resistance when they came to retake a city now in a ruinous state. All efforts by the European powers to eject the Turks from Edirne on a permanent basis failed, and under the Bucharest Treaty of 10 August 1913 Edirne was left to the Ottomans.

Frontier city

Between 1920 and 1922, in the wake of the First World War, Edirne spent over two years under Greek occupation. Following the Mudanya Armistice a Turkish army entered Edirne on 25 November 1922. Finally the Lausanne Treaty of 24 July 1923 turned Edirne into a frontier town on the border with Greece and Bulgaria.

THE BUILDINGS

Despite nearly two centuries of largely man-made devastation, Edirne still retained many of its Turkish monuments. While the first Ottoman capital Bursa is renowned today largely for its early Ottoman architecture, the second capital Edirne represents the entire spectrum of Ottoman architecture over the centuries. Even though its own role as capital ended in the mid-fifteenth century, it was bedecked over subsequent centuries with buildings representing the greatest eras of Ottoman architecture.

Yıldırım Bayezid Mosque

The oldest Turkish building in Edirne, dating from 1397-1400, this mosque was built on the foundations of an earlier cruciform Byzantine church. It has a small central dome surrounded by four vaults.

Eski Mosque

Construction of this mosque began in 1403 by Emir Süleyman Çelebi, and was completed in 1414 by Sultan Mehmed Çelebi. Its architect was Hacı Alaeddin of Konya. The square building with nine small domes and four pillars is of the ulu mosque type. It is constructed of ashlar stone, and the portico is built of alternate courses of stone and brick. One of its most interesting features are the large inscriptions.

Muradiye Mosque

This mosque founded by Sultan Murad II in 1436 is one of the finest examples of mosques with secondary areas off the central prayer hall. While the exterior is severe, the interior is decorated with superb examples of fifteenth century Ottoman decorative art, in the form of tiles covering all but the north wall, beautiful stencilled decoration on the intrados of the large arch linking the two central domes, the magnificent mihrap niche and the minber.

Üç Şerefeli Mosque

This mosque was also founded by Murad II and constructed between 1438 and 1447. It marks the transition between early and classical Ottoman architecture. A transverse plan is used here in Turkish architecture for the first time. One of its four minarets has three balconies, another two balconies and the remaining two have a single balcony each. The minarets are richly decorated with stalactite carving, reeding and spiral motifs. Separate spiral staircases cleverly intertwined lead up to each of the balconies in the first minaret, which gives the mosque its name - Üç Şerefeli, meaning Three Balconied. The courtyard is surrounded by colonnades with slightly pointed arches and contains a *şadırvan* (ablution fountain).

Sultan Bayezid Mosque complex

When Sultan Bayezid II set out to conquer the forts of Kilia and Akkerman in Moldavia and Bessarabia he halted in Edirne to get in military supplies, and on 23 May 1484 the foundations were laid for a mosque and large *külliye* (complex) consisting of *şifahane* (hospital), *medrese* (college), *imaret* (public kitchen), *tabhane* (guest house), *hamam* (baths), and flour mill on the banks of the Tunca river. The project also included a bridge over the river.

At a time when in Europe the mentally ill were believed to be under the influence of the devil, and frequently burnt at the stake, patients in Bayezid's hospital were treated with music therapy. The hospital staff included ten singers and musicians playing the ney, violin, santur and ud. Certain modes of Turkish music were found to be particularly beneficial, among them neva, rast, dügah, segah, çargah and buselik. As well as music another form of therapy involved the scent of flowers.

This mosque numbers among the greatest monuments of Ottoman Turkish architecture. Designed by the architect Hayreddin, it has a single dome 21 metres in diameter over the prayer hall, and nearly a hundred smaller domes over the buildings of the complex.

Selimiye Mosque

This mosque was built between 1569 and 1575 by Mimar Sinan for Sultan Selim II, and Mimar Sinan described it as his masterpiece. It has four minarets, each with three balconies, and these graceful minarets set at each corner around the central dome are visible from a great distance outside the city.

The 31.5 metre diameter dome rests on eight pillars set back against the walls, so creating an unbroken soaring central space. The eloquent unity of the interior, visible in entirety at a glance, is remarkable. The clear silhouette of the exterior is dominated by the dome.

Selimiye Mosque is also celebrated for the perfection of its marble carving, tiles and calligraphic decoration. In particular the marble carving of the minber has never been surpassed. The mihrap wall, royal gallery and the pediments of all the lower course windows are decorated with beautiful tiling, the finest in colour and composition being the large tile panels on the mihrap wall. The stencil decoration on the ceiling of the lower part of the royal gallery is also of especial note.

An intricately carved marble şadırvan stands in the cloistered courtyard.

Edirne Palace

The earliest palace in Edirne was built by Murad I. In 1450 Sultan Murad II started building a new palace on a large site on the west bank of the Tunca, and following his death in 1451 this palace was completed by his son Mehmed II.

One of the most important palace buildings was the Cihannüma Kasır, a seven storey structure on whose top floor was an octagonal chamber containing an ornamental pool in the centre. Next to Cihannüma was the Kum Kasır, which had a hamam with a spiral ribbed dome.

Behind the Cihannüma Kasır was a rectangular *maksem* (a water distribution structure) over a vaulted basement. Water from the *su terazisi* (water towers placed in valleys which acted on the principal of hydraulic levels and served as inverted siphons) filled tanks in the maksem, from which it was distributed in six directions. In the second half of the sixteenth century a prayer terrace was built at the palace.

Much of the palace was badly damaged during the Russian occupation which began on 22 August 1829. When Sultan Abdülaziz made his state visit to Europe in 1867, he travelled on the Sultaniye yacht for the outward journey but returned by land. Since the original plan had been for him to travel via Edirne, the Cihannüma Kasır was repaired and some additions made in preparation for his arrival. But instead the sultan travelled from Belgium via Coblenz, Prussia, Vienna and Budapest by road, and made the rest of the journey by steam ship along the Danube, across the Black Sea and through the Bosphorus.

In 1875 when news arrived that the Russian army was on its way to capture Edirne, the city's governor Cemil Paşa blew up the ammunition dump near the palace to prevent it falling into Russian hands. The explosions lasted for three or four days, endangering the city and demolishing the 425 year-old palace.

When the Roman emperor Hadrian journeyed to the eastern provinces of his empire in 123-124 he built a magnificent castle at Edirne, which had been named Hadrianopolis after himself. This castle was still standing until the mid-nineteenth century. Between 1866 and 1870 it was demolished and the stone used to build a hospital, school, government buildings and an army barracks. Of the four corner towers only one survived, transformed into a clock tower.

Bridges

Edirne is a city of many bridges, most of them spanning the Tunca. These stone bridges, mentioned in many folk songs, reflect the spatial and monumental concepts of contemporary Ottoman architecture. Those within the city are an integral part of the urban texture. The imposing beauty of Edirne's bridges, some of which outside the city are the work of Mimar Sinan, were never matched elsewhere.

The oldest of these bridges dates from the reign of the Byzantine emperor Michael Palaeologus (1261-1282). This 27 arch bridge was renovated by Gazi Mihal Bey in 1420 and thereafter known after him. In 1640 Kemankeş Kara Mustafa Paşa constructed a pointed arched baldachin, the Tarih Köşk, on the bridge.

In 1451 the twelve arch Şahabettin Paşa Bridge (also known as Saraçhane Bridge) was constructed. This was followed in 1452 by the Fatih Bridge, the Bayezid Bridge built in 1488 by Mimar Hayreddin, the Saray (Kanuni) Bridge built in 1560 by Mimar Sinan, Ekmekçizade Ahmed Paşa Bridge built in 1608-1615 by Sedefkar Mehmed Ağa and the Meriç (Yeni) Bridge at the confluence of the Meriç and Arda rivers between 1842 and 1847. These are the most notable of Edirne's historic bridges.

Kervansarays

*Kervansaray*s (caravanserais) were the hotels of their day, providing accommodation and stabling for merchants and travellers. One of the most interesting examples of classical

Ottoman kervansarays is Rüstem Paşa Kervansaray, built by Mimar Sinan for Süleyman the Magnificent's celebrated grand vezir Rüstem Paşa. It consists of a central rectangular courtyard surrounded by colonnades, behind which are the rooms. Along one of the exterior walls it has a row of shops which provided income for the institution.

Ekmekçioğlu Ahmed Paşa Kervansaray was built in 1609 by Ekmekçioğlu Ahmed Paşa, finance minister to Sultan Ahmed I, on that sultan's orders. Its architects were Sedefkar Mehmed Ağa and Hacı Şaban of Edirne.

Vernacular architecture

Edirne houses were timber framed with stone foundations, and the exterior often plastered. They had broad eaves and jutting bays supported by series of struts. The entrance was set back slightly in the centre of the main façade.

One room facing Mecca was usually set aside as a prayer room. All the living rooms had fitted cupboards where linen and household ware of all kinds were kept. There were jugs, cups, bowls and plates for serving preserves, confectionery, sherbet and syrups, embroidered towels and other linen, basins and ewers. Rooms where guests were received had shelves along the walls on which the family's most treasured pottery and porcelain plates, bowls and jugs would be displayed, and alcoves containing several shelves known as *katlı raf* were similarly used to display pretty bowls, *gülabdan* (rosewater sprinklers) and vases.

Since Edirne's winters could be extremely cold, the walls were thick to provide insulation and the rooms contained fireplaces either set into the walls or protruding from the exterior walls in the form of conical towers.

The Edirne house plan, which was adopted throughout the Balkans, was characterised by a central gallery room known as a *hayat* off which the other rooms opened, a feature of all houses from the most humble to the grandest. At one end the hayat jutted out over the garden, supported by posts 1.5-2 metres in height. This end of the hayat was raised slightly from the floor level of the rest of the gallery and surrounded by wooden divans.

Large houses had separate courtyards for the *harem* (the private part of the house reserved for the family and female guests) and *selamlık* (where the master of the household received guests and carried out his business affairs) sections. These contained marble fountains, sometimes small pools and vine shaded arbours. A small door linked the harem and selamlık courtyards.

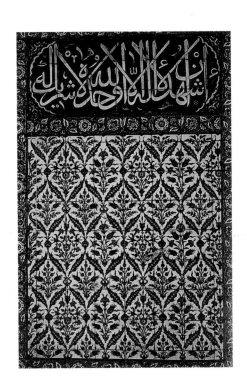

COMMERCIAL LIFE

Edirne was a major centre of trade which enjoyed centuries of prosperity. The fortress like bazaars known as *bedesten* where traders in jewellery and other precious goods had their shops was guarded by a watchman at night. The revival of trade in the eastern Mediterranean in the fifteenth century was the main factor in Edirne's economic development.

Wheat, barley, maize and other agricultural staples shipped from Egypt, the Aegean islands, İzmir and other western Anatolian cities arrived at the port of Enez, where they were loaded onto smaller ships and sent up river to Edirne. In addition rice from Filibe (Plovdiv) arrived via the Meriç river and was sent from here to Istanbul.

In the seventeenth century merchants arriving with their caravans from Iran would market these goods in Edirne, load up with new purchases and continue on into the Balkans. Goods from Europe were also found in the markets of Edirne, and from here European merchants returned home with beeswax and leather goods. Venetian and French merchants came here to purchase silks from Bursa and woollens from Ereğli.

Bazaars

Numerous commercial buildings were constructed in Edirne to provide accommodation, storage and retail premises for merchants and shopkeepers as the economy of the city flourished. As well as bedestens for trading and storing valuable goods, there were hans where craftsmen and merchants could rent offices and workshops and bazaars. Rentals from these buildings provided revenues for the upkeep of the mosques, and paid for the food distributed to students, the poor and mosque personnel at the imarets.

Between 1417 and 1418 Sultan Mehmed I Çelebi founded a bedesten as an endowment for Eski Mosque. Built by Mimar Alaeddin, this 14 domed building consisted of a row of shops around the outside and 36 vaulted rooms inside. Its walls were of red and white ashlar stone.

Ali Paşa Çarşısı was a bazaar of 130 shops built by Mimar Sinan for Hersekli Semiz Ali Paşa in 1569. The bazaar was 300 metres long and had six gates.

An *arasta* (open bazaar) consisting of 124 shops was founded as an endowment for Selimiye Mosque by Murad III (1574-1595) and built by the architect Davut Ağa. The arasta was 255 metres in length with 73 arches.

Tradesmen and shopkeepers

Edirne attracted a large population of craftsmen, including leather workers, saddlers, harness makers, felt makers, shoe makers, weavers, spinners, silk thread makers and tailors. There were also large numbers of cook shops, kebab shops, grocers, bakers and butchers. The frequent presence of the court, notables and wealthy local citizens also meant that goldsmiths and jewellers were numerous.

Other groups of artisans included metalworkers such as iron and coppersmiths, dyers, cart and carriage makers, textile printers, rose oil makers and soap makers. Their shops were mainly on the ground floors of two or three storey buildings facing the streets, and in some cases consisted of rows of shops with upper storeys. Part of the tax revenues raised in Edirne provided income for public institutions.

CULTURAL LIFE

Door onto the West

At its height Edirne was one of the Ottoman Empire's most important cities, situated strategically on the military and economic transit routes into Europe. The westernised fashions of Istanbul were adopted with alacrity in Edirne, from which they spread into the Balkan territories of Turkey.

In the seventeenth century Edirne had a population of 350,000, making it Europe's fourth largest city after Istanbul, Paris and London. Subsequently the decline which had begun with the fire of 1745 gathered momentum with the series of enemy occupations during the nineteenth century (the Russian occupations of 1829 and 1878, Bulgarian occupation of 1913 and Greek occupation of 1920-1922). During the war with Russia in 1828-1829 a large part of the Muslim population migrated, and their place was taken by Christians from outlying villages.

The local gipsy community were without doubt the most vivacious of Edirne's inhabitants. The men made a living tinning copper and as carters, while most of the women were peddlers who sold their wares from door to door. The gipsies, who were Muslims, were also popular musicians with their own distinctive style. They played such instruments as drums, zurna, clarinet, kanun, darbuka, def (tamborine), ud and cümbüş.

At the end of the nineteenth century the Turkish and Muslim population was 79,000, Greek 77,000, Armenian 5000, Bulgarian 32,000 and Jewish 9000.

Edirne was a subprovince known as a *paşa sancağı* attached to the Beylerbeyi of Rumeli until the 1840s, when it became a province.

Kırkpınar oil wrestling

Kırkpınar, the site of the famous oil wrestling tournament, is a word meaning Forty Springs, and is thought to have been named after forty Turkish warriors who formed the vanguard of the first Ottoman crossing over the Çanakkale (Dardanelles) Strait into Europe in the fourteenth century.

The Turkish principalities of Aydın and Saruhan who had assisted the Byzantines in quelling rebellious Byzantine fortresses and cities in the European territories of the empire, later made a habit of raiding these regions, and the Byzantine emperor sought an alliance with the Ottomans, who were becoming an increasingly powerful and expanding force in Anatolia.

Orhan Gazi had no objection to taking advantage of this situation by aiding the Byzantines against rival Turkish principalities. While the latter were intent only on short term gains, and always returned to Anatolia after their incursions, his aim was different. Orhan Gazi intended to gain a foothold on European soil and to expand his budding Ottoman Empire westwards.

Orhan Gazi sent a force under Süleyman Bey to take one of the Byzantine forts in Rumelia. Süleyman Bey crossed the Çanakkale Strait on two rafts with forty picked warriors, and in a surprise attack towards dawn took the fort of Kallipolis (Gelibolu). With reinforcements who crossed the strait later, he went on to lead his forces against a series of fortresses in the region.

The forty trusty warriors who formed the vanguard of this force were all master wrestlers, and whenever the army stopped to camp they held wrestling matches. When they arrived at a meadow some distance away from Hadrianopolis, they again organised a tournament, at which one pair of wrestlers resumed a match that had remained unfinished at the previous tournament. The match happened to coincide with the spring festival of Hıdrellez. Evening fell, but still neither of the pair had beaten the other. They continued in the darkness, and eventually towards midnight both died of exhaustion. They were buried in the meadow here, and the army marched on to Hadrianopolis the next day.

Time passed and Orhan Gazi had died to be succeeded by his son Murad I. Hadrianople was now in Turkish hands, and had become known as Edirne. The surviving warrior wrestlers decided to erect stones over the graves of their two heroic fellows. When they arrived at the meadow they found a stream of crystal clear water gushing from forty springs, and named the meadow Kırkpınar. The meadow of Kırkpınar lies about 25 kilometres west of Edirne, and is today inside the Greek frontier.

When Murad I made Edirne his capital, he established a lodge to train archers, *cirit* players (an equestrian game played between two teams throwing a javelin) and wrestlers, and at the same time it became traditional for a wrestling tournament to be held at Kırkpınar each year. About three weeks before Hıdrellez the steward of the tournament, known as the Kırkpınar Ağa, would send candles with red bases to the cities, towns and villages of the region, and these would be hung from the ceilings of coffee houses as messages to wrestlers of particular note living in those neighbourhoods. This gave rise to the expression, 'Were you invited with a red based candle?', in reference to someone who turns up uninvited.

Two weeks before the tournament local villagers would begin erecting stalls for tradesmen and shaded arbours around the wrestling field for the spectators. Tradesmen would rent the stalls to sell their wares, food and drinks.

A week before the tournament the steward would supervise the erection of tents for the wrestlers and guests. Cauldrons and pans would be brought to the meadow, and the cooks would begin their preparations for the three days of feasting and entertainment to come.

The tournament commenced three days prior to Hıdrellez. Two or three of the oldest and most respected wrestlers would be appointed as referees who watched the matches with the steward from his own tent. The last day was set aside for the wrestling match between the first and second master wrestlers, and generally the tournament would draw to an end on the eve of Hıdrellez.

Edirne red and Edirne work

Edirnekâri is a type of painted decoration done on wood. From the fourteenth century onwards this decoration was applied to ceilings, doors, and shelves in the wooden houses of Edirne, and to furniture such as cupboards, clocks, chests, pen cases and boxes. Inside the boxes gilt *tuğra* (imperial ciphers) and other motifs were executed.

The designs of Edirnekâri consisted primarily of flowers, leaves and fruits, executed with fine craftsmanship in paints noted for their durability.

The single flowers or small sprays of flowers typical of this work until the seventeenth century were replaced in the eighteenth century by large bunches of flowers or flowers in vases.

At the same time designs of this type began to appear on leather book bindings, and the lacquered bindings for which Edirne was renowned therefore also became known as Edirnekâri.

In the eighteenth century Edirne became famous for a red dye known as Turkey red or Edirne red (rouge d'Adrianople in Europe). Cotton fabrics dyed in this colour were also known as Edirne red.

The original painted decoration known Edirnekâri work survived until the mid-nineteenth century, and pieces of great beauty were produced by masters of the art.

Festivals

Until the sixteenth century all imperial festivals in celebration of events such as victories, circumcisions of royal princes and marriages of royal princesses were held in Edirne. Although from the sixteenth century onwards Istanbul took over this role, Mehmed IV held a festival in Edirne in 1675 to celebrate the circumcision of his sons.

The first festival in Edirne was held to celebrate the capture and execution of Mustafa the Pretender by Murad II. The same sultan held splendid circumcision feasts here for his sons Alaeddin and Mehmed II, and in 1444 organised a festival in celebration of the *Ramazan bayram* (the holiday marking the end of this month of fasting) consisting mainly of sports displays and lasting three days and three nights. In 1450 a festival which continued for an unprecedented three months was held in celebration of the marriage of Murad's son Şehzade Mehmed to Sitti Hatun.

In 1457, four years after Istanbul had been conquered and proclaimed capital, Mehmed II the Conqueror held a festival in Edirne to celebrate the circumcision of his sons Şehzade Bayezid and Şehzade Mustafa. As well as sports events and other accustomed entertainments, it featured discussions and debates between scholars.

In addition to these, circumcision celebrations were held in Edirne in 1472 for Mehmed's sons Cem Sultan and Şehzade Abdullah, and in 1480 for Selim, Şehinşah, Mahmud, Alem, Korkud, Ahmet and Oğuz Han.

Undoubtedly the most spectacular of all these festivals was that organised in 1674 by Mehmed IV who lived in Edirne for most of his reign. This was to celebrate the circumcision of his 12 year-old son Mustafa (the future Mustafa II) and his two year-old son Ahmed (the future Ahmed III), and the wedding of his 17 year-old daughter Hatice Sultan to his vezir and companion Mustafa Paşa. The feasting and celebrations for the circumcision lasted 16 days, for the wedding 19 days, and are among the most colourful pages in Edirne's history.

Preparations for the festivities began six months in advance. Extravagantly decorated standards known as *nahıl*, artificial gardens carried on floats, and figures of animals made of sugar were traditional features of the parades. Acrobats, illusionists, snake charmers, shadow players, puppeteers and many other performers entertained the crowds and horse races, archery contests, cirit matches, sword fights and wrestling matches were held.

In the eighteenth century country excursions and picnics became a favourite recreation of the urban population. Every city had its attractive meadows and parks in the vicinity, and in Edirne it was the orchards and meadows along the Meriç river where the people gathered on summer holidays to enjoy the green surroundings, the view of the river, and chatting to their companions.

PROLOGUE

The city which had been known in antiquity variously as Odrisya, Odrysai, Odrusa, Odrintsi, Odrysa, Orestia, Orestias, Oreistias, Orestas and Uscudama, became the Hadrianopolis of the Roman emperor Hadrian, also known as Adrianoupolis, Adrianopolis, Adrinople and Andrinople. The Ottomans were equally generous with their versions of the name, calling the city Edrinus, Edrune, Edrenos, Edreneboli, Edrinabolu, Edrene and Endriye.

After handing on its role as capital to Istanbul, the city guarded the door into the Balkans. This city was the Edirne of the Turks.

View of Edirne.

Photograph: Abdullah Frères, circa 1890.

Edirne flooded by the Tunca.   Photograph: D. Michailides, circa 1890.

Edirne flooded by the Tunca.

Photograph: D. Michailides, circa 1890.

View of Edirne.

Anonymous, 1910.

View of Edirne.

Photograph: D. Michailides, circa 1890.

View of Edirne.

Photograph: D. Michailides, circa 1890.

View of Edirne.

Photograph: D. Michailides, circa 1890.

View of Edirne.

Photograph: D. Michailides, circa 1890.

Edirne Government House and Police Department.

Photograph: D. Michailides, circa 1890.

View of Edirne.

Postcard.

The neighbourhood of Kaleiçi and Selimiye Mosque.

Photograph: F. Fettah, circa 1920.

View of Edirne.

Postcard.

Edirne Government House and Police Department.

Postcard.

Environs of Taşlık in Edirne.

Photograph: F. Fettah, circa 1920.

Yıldırım Yeni Imaret.

Photograph: F. Fettah, circa 1920.

Edirne from the east.

Photograph: F. Fettah, circa 1920.

Edirne from the north.   Postcard.

View of Edirne.

Postcard.

View of Edirne.

Photograph: F. Fettah, circa 1920.

Selimiye Mosque, Üç Şerefeli Mosque, Eski Mosque and the clock tower.

Photograph: F. Fettah, circa 1920.

View of Edirne.   Postcard.

View of Edirne.

Postcard.

Panoramic view of Edirne (this is in fact five separate photographs joint together).

Photograph: F. Fettah, circa 1920.

Ruins of the Old Palace in Edirne.

Photograph: M. Şevki, circa 1930.

Edirne Railway Station.

Postcard.

Edirne High School for Boys.

Military Office.

Photograph: D. Michailides, circa 1890.

Inauguration of the *su terazisi* (water balance tower) constructed in Kaleiçi after the great fire of 1903.   Postcard.

Water balance tower.

Postcard.

A motorcar in front of Canik Hotel.

Postcard.

Canik Hotel.   Postcard.

Karaağaç Railway Station.   Photograph: F. Fettah, circa 1930.

Paşa Gate.

Postcard.

Greek School for Girls.

Postcard.

Field Marshal's Office.   Postcard.

French Hospital. Postcard.

Reserves Office.

Postcard.

Hacı Adil Bey Fountain.

Municipality Building.   Postcard.

Edirne Junior School for Girls.

Photograph: M. Şevki, circa 1930.

Edirne Teachers' Training College for Men.

Photograph: M. Şevki, circa 1930.

Edirne Teachers' Training College for Women.

Photograph: M. Şevki, circa 1930.

Military Hospital.

Photograph: F. Fettah, circa 1920.

Reşadiye Garden.   Postcard.

Government House.

Photograph: D. Michailides, circa 1890.

Meriç Bridge.   Postcard.

Meriç Bridge.   Postcard.

Meriç Bridge.

Photograph: M. Şevki, circa 1930.

Meriç Bridge.

Photograph: Sébah & Joaillier, circa 1890.

Meriç Bridge.

Photograph: M. Şevki, circa 1930.

Saraçhane Bridge.

Postcard.

Tunca Bridge.   Postcard.

Tunca Bridge.

Postcard.

Saray Bridge.

Photograph: F. Fettah, circa 1930.

Cows by a bridge.

Photograph: D. Michailides, circa 1890.

Tunca Bridge.

Photograph: D. Michailides, circa 1890.

River Meriç.

Postcard.

Confluence of the Meriç and Arda rivers with the Tunca.

Photograph: M. Şevki, circa 1920.

Banks of the Meriç.

Photograph: D. Michailides, circa 1890.

Steps leading down to the river Tunca from Evliya Kasım Paşa Mosque, and fishermen letting out their nets.

Photograph: M. Şevki, 1929.

River Meriç.

Photograph: D. Michailides, circa 1890.

Boating on the River Tunca.

Photograph: D. Michailides, circa 1890.

The Tunca and Bayezid II Mosque.

Photograph: M. Şevki, circa 1930.

River Meriç.

Photograph: M. Şevki, circa 1930.

Hamidiye Caddesi.

Postcard.

A street in Edirne.

Photograph: D. Michailides, circa 1890.

Saraçlar Caddesi.

Photograph: F. Fettah, circa 1930.

Mimar Sinan Caddesi.

Photograph: F. Fettah, circa 1930.

Mumcular Caddesi.

Postcard.

Abacılar Başı Caddesi.

Postcard.

A street in Edirne.

Anonymous, circa 1900.

Meriç Bridge.

Photograph: F. Fettah, circa 1920.

Abacılar Başı Caddesi.

Postcard.

A street in Edirne.

Hamidiye Caddesi.   Postcard.

A street in Edirne.

Photograph: D. Michailides, circa 1890.

A neighbourhood in Edirne.

Photograph: D. Michailides, circa 1890.

A street in Edirne.

Photograph: D. Michailides, circa 1890.

Edirne Palace, Adalet Kasır and köşks. To the right is a photographer preparing to take a photograph.   Postcard.

Edirne Palace. Postcard.

Edirne Palace.   Postcard.

Adalet Kasır at Sarayiçi in Edirne and Fatih Bridge.

Photograph: D. Michailides, circa 1890.

A shepherd and his flock in the environs of Edirne.

Photograph: Ali Sami Aközer, circa 1880.

A wayside water fountain near Edirne. Photograph: Ali Sami Aközer, circa 1880.

A dance from the Edirne area.

Postcard.

Soldiers at Edirne.   Postcard.

Soldiers at Edirne.

Postcard.

Military College.   Postcard.

Soldiers at Edirne.   Postcard.

Mülkiye İdadi School.

Postcard.

Artillery soldiers in Edirne.

Postcard.

Government House.   Postcard.

Barracks.   Postcard.

Bulgarian children at Karaağaç.   Postcard.

Bulgarian children at Karaağaç.

Postcard.

Hürriyet Garden.   Postcard.

Emin Pehlivan, a wrestler
of Çömlek village.

Postcard.

Postcard.

134

Two famous wrestlers.
On the left is Adalı Halil,
and on the right Kurtdereli Mehmed.
When Field Marshal Ahmed Paşa was
deputy governor in Edirne he heard
that these two wrestlers had fallen out.
He mediated a reconciliation and
had this photograph taken.
A wrestling match between the two
was organised at Sarayiçi in Edirne.
Despite these endeavours, the two
wrestlers never met again.

Photograph: D. Joseph, 1902.

A Bulgarian from Ahi Çelebi, a Muslim *sipahi* (horseman) from Filibe (Plovdiv) and a Bulgarian from Koyuntepe.

Photograph: Pascal Sébah, 1873.

A Greek artisan from Edirne, Muslim sipahi and shopkeeper.

Photograph. Pascal Sébah, 1873.

A peasant woman and man from Manastır (Monastir) and a Bulgarian woman from Üsküdar.

Photograph: Pascal Sébah, 1873.

Edirne Government House and the Selimiye and Sultan Bayezid mosques.

Postcard.

A neighbourhood in Edirne.

Photograph: D. Michailides, circa 1890.

Edirne Imaret.

Postcard.

Edirne Imaret and surrounding buildings.

Photograph: D. Michailides, circa 1890.

Eski Mosque.   Postcard.

Darülhadis Mosque.   Postcard.

144

Darülhadis Mosque.   Postcard.

Sultan Bayezid Mosque complex.

Postcard.

Sultan Bayezid Mosque.

Photograph: M. Şevki, circa 1930.

Sultan Bayezid Mosque complex.

Photograph: Abdullah Frères, circa 1890.

Eski Mosque in Edirne.

Photograph: D. Michailides, circa 1890.

Kasım Paşa Mosque.

Evliya Kasım Paşa Mosque and Imaret on the banks of the Tunca.   Photograph: D. Michailides, circa 1890.

The şadırvan at Selimiye Mosque.

Photograph: Sébah & Joaillier, 1889.

Selimiye Mosque.

Photograph: Gülmez Frères, circa 1890.

After the Bulgarian occupation of 26 March 1913, many postcards depicting Edirne were printed in Sofya. One of these cards depicts Bulgarian soldiers in front of the şadırvan of Selimiye Mosque.

Postcard.

Selimiye Mosque.

Postcard.

Selimiye Mosque.

Photograph: M. Şevki, circa 1930.

Interior of Selimiye Mosque.

Postcard.

Şadırvan of Selimiye Mosque.

Photograph: F. Fettah, circa 1930.

Selimiye Mosque and Edirne.

Photograph: F. Fettah, circa 1930.

Saray Bridge.

Photograph: M. Şevki, circa 1930.

Saray Bridge.

Postcard.

Selimiye Mosque, Üç Şerefeli Mosque and the clock tower.

Postcard.

Üç Şerefeli Mosque.

Photograph: M. Şevki, circa 1930.

Edirne and Üç Şerefeli Mosque.

Anonymous, circa 1880.

The clock tower.

Postcard.

The clock tower.

Photograph: D. Michailides, circa 1895.

THE PHOTOGRAPHERS

Abdullah Frères

(Viçen 1820-1902, Hovsep 1830-1908, Kevork 1839-1918)

The three Abdullah brothers took over the studio of the German chemist Rabach in Beyazıt in 1856. They later sold this studio to Andreomenos and opened a new studio in Péra where hundreds of young photographers received their early training. In guide books of the time the Abdullah Frères studio was recommended to tourists visiting Istanbul, along with such famous city sights as the Bosphorus and historic monuments like Haghia Sophia.

In 1863 they took a portrait photograph of Sultan Abdülaziz for a medallion which was struck by the Empress Augusta of Germany. The sultan issued an edict awarding them the title of Imperial Photographers to the Court, a title which they retained during the reign of Abdülhamid II.

The Abdullah brothers took portraits of many famous figures who visited the Ottoman Empire, and in 1886 at the request of Tevfik Paşa, khedive of Egypt, they opened a branch studio in Cairo.

At the end of the century they sold their studio to Sébah & Joaillier.

Ali Sami Aközer (1866-1936)

Aközer was born in Ruse, and later moved to Istanbul with his family, who settled in the district of Beylerbeyi just north of Üsküdar. Hence he was known as Ali Sami of Üsküdar. In 1886 he graduated from the artillery class of the Imperial Engineering School. Ali Sami was son-in-law of Servili Ahmed Emin, head art teacher at the Engineering School, where he himself taught art and photography until 1908. During this time he also gave lessons in photography to Abdülhamid II's son Burhanettin Efendi.

Üsküdarlı Ali Sami was an excellent draughtsman and watercolourist as well as photographer. In 1892 he was promoted to the rank of adjutant major. After the declaration of the 1908 constitution he left the army and taught art at a high school in Trabzon on the eastern Black Sea coast. He died in Istanbul in 1836.

Gülmez Frères

The three Gülmez brothers are best known for their photographs of the countryside around Istanbul. They opened a studio in Péra in 1870 and were awarded the title of Photographers by Appointment to the Sultan and a medal. They received medals of honour at the 1887 Florence Exhibition and the 1893 Chicago Exhibition. Their studio closed down at the end of the nineteenth century and all the photographs were sold to Aşil Samancı.

Basile Kargopoulo

This Ottoman Greek photographer opened a studio at No 311 Grand' Rue de Péra close to the Russian Embassy in 1850. Subsequently he moved to No 417 on the same street. He opened a second studio in Edirne, then a busy garrison town, in partnership with E. Foscolo.

In 1895 the Istanbul studio moved to No. 4 Tünel Meydanı, the square at the southern end of Grand' Rue de Péra. Foscolo left the Edirne studio which Kargopoulo then ran single-handed. His Istanbul studio remained open until 1912.

Kargopoulo's Istanbul scenes and panoramas are valuable documents of the city. He also did portrait photography, keeping a large wardrobe of costumes in which young men could dress up to have their photographs taken.

He photographed royal palaces and köşks, Bosphorus scenes and street vendors selling such wares as fish, vegetables, *simit* (bread rings sprinkled with sesame seeds) and *şerbet* (sweetened fruit juices). It was these photographs which won him renown.

He was awarded the title of Photographer to His Majesty the Sultan by Sultan Abdülmecid, and enjoyed the patronage of the sultans for many years. He was appointed private photographer to Murad V during his brief reign of a few months in 1876. The title was retracted by Sultan Abdülhamid II when it was discovered that he kept a photograph of the deposed Murad V on his studio wall, but the title was soon reinstated.

Michailides, D.

Michailides was one of the photographers who had studios in Edirne in the nineteenth century. This Greek photographer continued to work here into the early twentieth century.

Sébah & Joaillier
(Pascal Sebah (1823-1886) / Policarpe Joaillier)

Pascal Sébah was born in Istanbul where he opened a studio on Postacılar Caddesi in Péra in 1857, naming it El Chark Société Photographic. He later moved to No. 439 Grand' Rue de Péra adjoining the Russian Embassy (which was then inside the building known today as Narmanlı Yurdu). He went into partnership with a Frenchman named A. Laroche.

Pascal Sébah took all the photographs of Ottoman costumes for the Ottoman Exhibition in Vienna in 1873. He was awarded the Osmanî and third class Mecidî medals and medals at the Vienna, Philadelphia and Paris exhibitions in 1873, 1876 and 1878 respectively. His panoramas, stereoscopes and scenes of Istanbul, Bursa, the Aegean coast, Athens, Egypt and Libya earned him an international reputation. The famous Ottoman painter, Osman Hamdi Bey, used photographs by Pascal Sébah as studies for some of his paintings.

At the end of 1873 he opened a branch studio next to the famous Shepard's Hotel in Cairo.

Pascal Sébah died in Istanbul in 1886, but his studio lived on, and in 1888 was renamed Sébah & Joaillier.

Photographs of an army officer with his three children taken in the studio of the Edirne photographer Aram Bardizban.

Aram Bardizban
PHOTOGRAPHE
ANDRINOPLE

The back of Aram Bardizban's
studio mounts printed by Wachtl
in Vienna.

The back of the studio mount of Basile Kargopoulo, a well known Istanbul photographer. The design includes the medals which he received from the Ottoman government and at international photography competitions. The address of the Istanbul studio is given at the bottom of the mount, where it also writes that there is a branch of the studio in Edirne.

The back of the studio mount used
by Kargopoulo after he went into
partnership with the Edirne
photographer E. Foscolo.

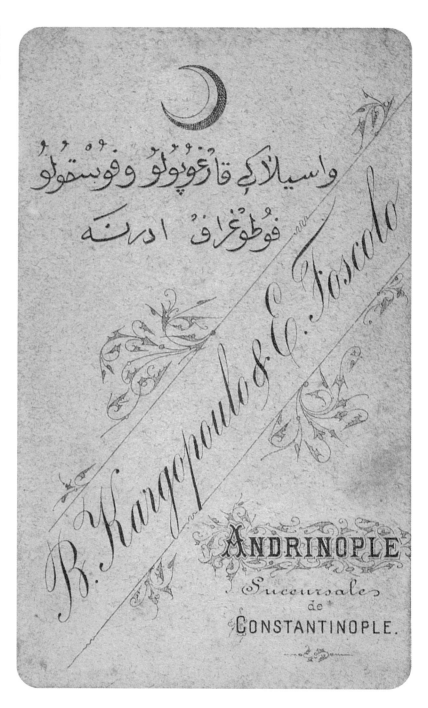

Stereoscope of Selimiye Mosque in Edirne. Stereoscopes were taken with special double lensed cameras and had to be looked at through special viewers. They took the form of positive images on glass or photographic paper. The double image creates a three-dimensional effect.

Photograph: Ali Sami Aközer, circa 1900.

BIBLIOGRAPHY

Arseven, Celal Esad, *Türk Sanatı*, Cem Yayınevi, Istanbul 1970.

Arseven, Celal Esad, *Sanat Ansiklopedisi*, Milli Eğitim Basımevi, Istanbul 1950.

Cerası, Maurice M., *Osmanlı Kenti*, Yapı Kredi Yayınları, Istanbul 1999.

Edirne'nin 600. Fetih Yıldönümü Armağan Kitabı, Türk Tarih Kurumu Basımevi, Ankara 1993.

Erhat, Azra, *Mitoloji Sözlüğü*, Remzi Kitabevi, Istanbul 1993.

Erzen, Afif, *İlkçağ Tarihinde Trakya*, Arkeoloji ve Sanat Yayınları, Istanbul 1994.

Faroqhi, Suraiya, *Osmanlı'da Kentler ve Kentliler*, Tarih Vakfı Yurt Yayınları, Istanbul 1993.

Heredotos, *Herodot Tarihi*, Remzi Kitabevi, Istanbul 1991.

Hamilton, Edith, *Mitologya*, Varlık Yayınları, Istanbul 1964.

İşli, Emin Nedret/Koz, M. Sabri (Editors), *Edirne: Serhattaki Payıtaht*, Yapı Kredi Yayınları, Istanbul 1998.

Kahraman, Atıf, *Osmanlı Devleti'nde Spor*, T.C. Kültür Bakanlığı Yayınları, Ankara 1995.

Karayel, M. Sami Adalı, *Halil ve Kızılcıklı Mahmut*, Ahmet Halit Kitabevi, Istanbul 1948.

Nutku, Özdemir, *IV. Mehmet'in Edirne Şenliği (1675)*, Türk Tarih Kurumu Basımevi, Ankara 1987.

Osman, Rıfat (Ed.: Ord. Prof. Dr. Süheyl Ünver), *Edirne Evleri*, Türkiye Turing ve Otomobil Kurumu, Istanbul 1976.

Osman, Rıfat (Ed.: Ord. Prof. Dr. Süheyl Ünver), *Edirne Sarayı*, Türk Tarih Kurumu Basımevi, Ankara 1989.

Özdeş, Gündüz, *Türk Çarşıları*, Tepe Yayıncılık, Ankara 1998.

Tuğlacı, Pars, *Osmanlı Şehirleri*, Milliyet Gazetesi, Istanbul 1985.

Umar, Bilge, *Türkiye'deki Tarihsel Adlar*, İnkılap Kitabevi, Istanbul 1993.

Vilayetlerimizin Tarihi, Tifdruk Basımevi, Istanbul 1968.